A Life
Surrendered

June Kimmel

JOURNEY
FORTH™

Greenville, South Carolina

Front and Back Cover Photo Credits: Brand X Pictures

All Scripture is quoted from the Authorized King James Version.

A Life Surrendered
June Kimmel

Design by Rita Golden
Composition by Sarah Kurlowich

© 2007 BJU Press
Greenville, South Carolina 29614

ISBN 978-1-59166-728-5

15 14 13 12 11 10 9 8 7 6 5 4 3 2 1

To Jenny, Beth, and Jon
May your lives continue to reflect
a love and knowledge
of the surrendered Savior

TABLE OF CONTENTS

A Life Surrendered 3

WHO BEING GOD

His Riches 11
His Birthright 17

MADE IN THE LIKENESS OF MAN

His Early Years 27
His Humanity 33

MADE HIMSELF OF NO REPUTATION

A Humble Occupation 41
A Humble Ministry 47

TOOK UPON HIM THE FORM OF A SERVANT

A Servant's Heart 57
A Servant's Actions 63

OBEDIENT UNTO DEATH

The Surrender of the Son 71
The Surrender in Prayer 79

My Life Surrendered 87

Notes 95

A LIFE SURRENDERED

Lesson 1
A LIFE SURRENDERED

II Peter 3:18
But grow in grace and in the knowledge of our Lord
and Saviour Jesus Christ.

*I*f you were in a Bible study class with me for any length of time, you would hear me quote this verse. The Lord gave me this verse years ago as I struggled to understand His will for me. I was confronted with many questions for which I had no answers. I wanted to hide from the cares and burdens of this world. But through those days I learned a very important lesson—God is with me no matter where I am and no matter what I am facing. He showed me that the one thing I needed more than anything else in this world was to know Him better. My heart began to mend as I turned my focus to my Lord and His amazing grace.

About a year ago I began a study of biblical surrender. My first thoughts were of my responsibility to surrender to God. As I searched out the meaning of this word, I was drawn back to II Peter 3:18 and realized that to truly grasp the meaning of *surrender* I would have to study the life of the Lord Jesus. No man, even in his best attempts, could ever perfectly exemplify surrender. Only through a study of our Lord would I be able to envision a life surrendered.

Each lesson will be divided into two sections. We will consider different events in the life of the Lord Jesus that will show us how or what He surrendered by coming to this world to die as our Savior.

In the "Let This Mind Be in You" section, you will be challenged to apply these practical principles to your life. None of us will ever be able to master any of these areas, but we can challenge each other to surrender our lives more completely to our God.

Of all the studies I've taught throughout the years, I found this to be the most humbling. To fully convey the truths about our Lord is an overwhelming task. I feel inadequate to express what our Lord Jesus did for us in the past, what He is doing today, and what He promises to do in the future. But with His help and your prayers, I believe this may be one of the most challenging studies we could ever do together.

Definition of Surrender

The concept of surrendering, or submission, is contrary to the day in which we live. Everyone is challenged to strive for independence and self-exaltation. Equality has become such a demand that many have taken it beyond impartiality to superiority. Our society is driven with a need to take care of "number one" with no regard for the needs and feelings of others.

The word *surrender* is not found in the Bible, yet its pages are full of examples of and synonyms for surrender. *Surrender* means "the act of giving up one's person or possessions unto the authority of another or others or of relinquishing one's power, aims, or goals; to give over or resign to something."[1]

1. Use a dictionary to find the meaning of these Bible synonyms for *surrender*. Notice the slight differences in the definitions.

   Abandon— _____

   Relinquish— _____

   Submit— _____

   Subject— _____

   Yield— _____

2. List some characteristics of a person who surrenders. _____

_____

_____

Foundation of Surrender

God has a plan for each of us to follow. He desires that we surrender our lives to His complete control. This surrender begins with a realization of our need of a Savior. We must understand and accept that the Lord Jesus is the only One Who could pay for the debt of sin we owe to God. His death and resurrection paid the price of sin and brought the victory over sin. We each are responsible for our personal relationship to Jesus Christ. Is He your Savior? Has there been a time in your life when you realized you are a sinner in need of a Savior? Have you received the gift of salvation that He freely gives?

Study the following verses. If you have never trusted Christ as your Savior, follow the steps of these verses to receive the marvelous plan of salvation that God freely offers to all who believe and receive. If you have accepted this wonderful message, review it carefully and praise God for what He's already done in your life.

3. Romans 3:10—Who is righteous? _____

Romans 3:23—Who has sinned? _____

What standard cannot be attained? _____

Romans 6:23a—What wages or payment should I expect from my sin? _____

Romans 5:8—How has God shown His love for me? _____

_____

Romans 6:23b—What does God provide as a gift for me? _____

_____

Ephesians 2:8–9—What can I do to earn God's forgiveness?

_____

Romans 10:9–10, 13—What must I do to receive this precious gift of God? _____

_____

John 1:12—What do I become when I receive Christ as my Savior?_____

I John 1:9—Until I one day go to heaven to be with Him, I will still sin. But now as His child I can know His forgiveness as my heavenly Father. What must I do to take care of my daily sin?

_____

What does He promise He will do? _____

John 10:28–29—How enduring is this gift of salvation?_____

_____

Once we have received Jesus as our Savior, our relationship with Him has only begun. God desires to walk through this life with us. In fact, through His Word we can know the way He would have us live.

Let This Mind Be in You

Let this mind be in you, which was also in Christ Jesus. (Philippians 2:5)

As you go through this study, you will be challenged to apply the truths of surrender that you see in the life of the Lord Jesus. To simply understand them in light of the life of our Lord without applying them to our daily walk is futile. When Paul was inspired to write this passage in Philippians, he relayed a command to us first. We are to have a certain mindset that the Lord Jesus Himself patterns for us. But what was His mind? To see what is involved, we must look back to the verses that precede this verse.

That ye be likeminded, having the same love, being of one accord, of one mind. Let nothing be done through strife or vainglory; but in lowliness of mind let each esteem other better than themselves. Look not every man on his own things, but every man also on the things of others. (Philippians 2:2b–4)

6

In order for us to "let this mind be in" us, we must "keep thinking this"[2] way. These guidelines are to reflect our attitude because they are the Lord's attitudes.

4. List the seven attitudes given in these verses. How should you be demonstrating them in your daily life? When you have considered each attitude, put a check in the "Improvement Needed" box if this is an area that you need to develop with the Lord's help.

Attitude	Demonstrated in my life by . . .	Improvement needed?
_____ accord	Focusing on biblical truths and Christlike living as I fellowship and worship with other believers	
_____ mind		
_____ through strife		
Nothing done through _____		
Have _____ of mind		
Esteem others _____ _____		
Care for _____ _____		

Now we are ready to look at the next verses in Philippians. Verses 6–11 will prove that Jesus truly did possess these attitudes. Through the study of this outline God sets for us an example to follow—the life of the Lord Jesus. No man can ever give us the perfect pattern for a life surrendered to God, but through His Word we can learn about the Lord Jesus and understand what a surrendered life is. Join me now in this study of the life the Lord Jesus exemplifies for us.

WHO BEING GOD

Lesson 2
His Riches

Philippians 2:5–11
Let this mind be in you, which was also in Christ Jesus: who, being in the form of God, thought it not robbery to be equal with God: but made himself of no reputation, and took upon him the form of a servant, and was made in the likeness of men: and being found in fashion as a man, he humbled himself, and became obedient unto death, even the death of the cross. Wherefore God also hath highly exalted him, and given him a name which is above every name: that at the name of Jesus every knee should bow, of things in heaven, and things in earth, and things under the earth; and that every tongue should confess that Jesus Christ is Lord, to the glory of God the Father.

These verses in Philippians outline the life of surrender that Jesus lived. His purpose for coming to this earth was clear and focused. He was fully surrendered to the plan of redemption that God the Father and He, God the Son, had determined necessary to satisfy the debt of mankind's sin. The Lord Jesus willingly came to this sinful world to provide salvation. He came with a heart of humility. In everything He did, He illustrates this for us.

It is imperative that His heart of humility and surrender be ours if we are to be what He desires us to be. But what was the heart of Christ? How did He illustrate to us a life of surrender? What did He as God sacrifice to be our Savior? Let's see what He surrendered and what He asks of us.

His Preexistence

> Who, being in the form of God, thought it not robbery to be equal with God. (Philippians 2:6)

The foundation of all that the Bible proclaims is that Jesus is God. He didn't begin to exist that first Christmas night in Bethlehem. His "birth did not mark His origin, but only His appearance as a man on the stage of time."[1] He has always been—from eternity past. He proclaimed Himself to be the Creator as well as our Redeemer. These truths go far beyond our understanding; yet, as we read the Word of God, we see them often spoken of by the Lord Jesus Himself.

1. Let's study the following verses and note the words of our Lord as He proclaimed Who He is as the Eternal God.

   John 1:1—He was in the_____

   John 1:1—He was _____

   John 1: 2—He was with _____

   John 1:3—He _____all things.

   John 1:3—_____without Him.

   John 3:13—He came down from_____

   John 8:56–58—He existed before_____

   John 16:27–28—He came from _____
   to this world.

   John 17:5—Jesus' glory was with the Father before _____

   _____

   John 17:24—God the Father loved the Lord Jesus before the

   _____

His Riches

We often overlook the sacrifice Jesus made in His coming to this earth. We fail to consider the glorious heaven that He left and its contrast to this sin-cursed world. When Jesus came to this earth, He left all the riches of heaven behind. "He chose the oblivion of birth . . . humiliation of life."[2] Second Corinthians 8:9 states that although He was rich beyond all earthly riches, He willingly left it all for your sake and mine. He became poor for us that we might have the opportunity to know the joy of true riches through His life, death, and resurrection. The hymn "Ivory Palaces" communicates this picture for us.

Ivory Palaces

My Lord has garments so wondrous fine,
And myrrh their texture fills;
Its fragrance reached to this heart of mine,
With joy my being thrills.

His life had also its sorrows sore,
For aloes had a part;
And when I think of the cross He bore,
My eyes with teardrops start.

In garments glorious He will come,
To open wide the door;
And I shall enter my heav'nly home,
To dwell forevermore.

Out of the ivory palaces,
Into a world of woe,
Only His great eternal love
Made my Savior go.

—*Henry Barraclough*[3]

Jesus left the beauty of heaven for a sin-cursed world. The splendors of heaven are only briefly described for us in God's Word. "Heaven is a place and the eternal hope of the saved. Scripture describes it as a beautiful city where the redeemed will live for eternity."[4]

In Revelation 21:10–25, John gives us a description of the New Jerusalem, which the Lord will one day present to believers. Although it is described as "descending out of heaven from God" (Revelation 21:10), it no doubt is very similar to the splendor of heaven.

∾ **Time in the Word: Read Revelation 21:10–27.**

2. List the characteristics of the New Jerusalem from these verses in Revelation. _____

_____

_____

_____

3. Read these passages and note what will take place in heaven.

Passage	Life in Heaven
Revelation 14:13	
Revelation 15:3	
Revelation 19:1	
Revelation 22:3	
Revelation 22:4	

Thou Who Wast Rich
Thou who wast rich beyond all splendor,
All for love's sake becamest poor;
Thrones for a manger didst surrender,
Sapphire-paved courts for stable floor.

—*Frank Houghton*[5]

LET THIS MIND BE IN YOU

In John 14, we are given just a glimpse of what awaits us in heaven. Jesus told His disciples that He would soon leave them and gave them precious promises. Read the following verses to learn what Jesus shared with the disciples.

4. John 13:36—What was Jesus' response to Peter's asking to go with Him wherever He was going? _____

_____

5. John 13:37—What promise did Peter make to Jesus?_____

_____

6. John 13:38—Jesus questioned Peter's promise. In fact, what does Jesus tell Peter he would soon do?_____

7. John 14:1—After Peter responded to this answer, what did Jesus tell Peter and the disciples to do?_____

_____

8. John 14:2–3—What two things did Jesus promise His disciples that He would do? _____

_____

_____

9. This same promise is for you. How should this affect how you respond to all that happens to you today? _____

_____

10. John 14:6—What is the way to heaven? _____

_____

ᔎ Time to Memorize: Begin to memorize Philippians 2:5–8.

ᔎ Time for Prayer: During your prayer time today thank the Lord Jesus for leaving heaven to come to this earth to be your Savior. Ask Him to show you areas you need to surrender completely to Him.

From My Heart to Yours

My dad was a pastor throughout my years growing up. I heard him preach thousands of sermons from the time I was a little girl until I was married. Of all those sermons, one stands out as the best. We were living in northern Iowa; I was in sixth or seventh grade; the Vietnam War was in full swing. Like most families, our lives were touched by the death of a soldier—my cousin. He and his family lived in a little town in Michigan where my dad had pastored a few years earlier. When the call came asking my father to return to Michigan to do the funeral service, my dad was very sick. Sharing the grief in his family, Dad felt the Lord would have us go for the memorial services in spite of his condition. This made an incredible impact on me. How I prayed for my father as we made that long drive to Michigan. How I prayed as he stood in the pulpit behind that soldier's casket. I listened that day to my dad preach the most glorious sermon on heaven I have ever heard before or since. In spite of his weak, sick body, he, with incredible power, seemed to part the clouds and let us see heaven's splendor. We didn't know it then, but a few years later my dad was diagnosed with stomach cancer—probably the very thing that had made him so sick that day. What joy it must have been for him to enter his heavenly home that he'd given us a glimpse of that day!

Lesson 3
HIS BIRTHRIGHT

Philippians 2:5–6

Let this mind be in you, which was also in Christ Jesus: who, being in the form of God, thought it not robbery to be equal with God.

In our last lesson, we considered the riches of heaven that Jesus left behind when He came to this earth. All the splendor of heaven was His. Let's now study the fact that the Lord Jesus also left the loving fellowship and unity of God the Father and God the Holy Spirit. Although the Trinity is impossible for us to fully comprehend, Scripture describes the perfect, holy agreement of the Godhead. The Gospel of John clearly emphasizes the deity of the Lord Jesus and His exclusive relationship with God the Father and the Holy Spirit. "John refers to God as 'Father' 116 times, more than all the other gospels combined."[1]

> But I have a greater witness than that of John: for the works which the Father hath given me to finish, the same works that I do, bear witness of me, that the Father hath sent me. And the Father himself, which hath sent me, hath borne witness of me. Ye have neither heard his voice at any time, nor seen his shape. (John 5:36–37)

1. Match the passage with the truth about Jesus' relationship to God the Father and God the Holy Spirit.

_____ John 1:14   A. God the Father and Jesus are One.

_____ John 6:69   B. God the Father knows Jesus.

_____ John 10:17   C. Jesus is the only begotten of the Father.

_____ John 10:30   D. Jesus loves the Father.

_____ John 12:49–50   E. The Holy Spirit is sent by Jesus to convict us of sin and give comfort.

_____ John 14:31   F. God the Father loves Jesus.

_____ John 15:26   G. Jesus left this world to return to God the Father.

_____ John 16:7–11   H. Jesus is the Son of the living God.

_____ John 16:27–28   I. Jesus spoke the words of God the Father.

_____ John 10:15   J. God the Holy Spirit is sent from God to speak about Jesus.

John 17 records one of Jesus' prayers. This intercessory prayer "is often called the High Priestly Prayer of Christ, because He prays first for Himself and then for His own—the twelve, in verse 6, and all who will believe, in verse 20."[2] John, by inspiration, writes these words of Jesus to give us His heart's view of His relationship with the Father. These verses paint for us a vivid picture of Jesus' longing to be reunited with God the Father. He remembers the past and longs for His soon return to heaven.

❧ Time in the Word: Read John 17.

2. Read John 17 in its entirety to understand this prayer as a whole. Then consider the following:

What phrases of Jesus' prayer convey His loving relationship with the Father? _____

_____

_____

_____

_____

How did Jesus express His love for His followers? _____

_____

_____

_____

_____

His Birth

In the Old Testament we read of times the Lord Jesus appeared to man. These pre-incarnate appearances are called Christophanies. At these times, the Lord Jesus took on the form of man in order to minister to man. He was referred to as the "angel of the Lord," but the circumstances in each account indicate that it was the Lord Jesus Himself visiting these people.

Genesis 32:24–30—Jacob wrestled with the Angel of the Lord and declared that he had seen God face to face.

Exodus 3:1–6—God the Son spoke to Moses with the same description of Himself that He used in Matthew 22:32 when He was answering questions for the Sadducees.

Joshua 5:13–15—Joshua stood in the presence of sword-bearing deity.

Judges 6:11–22—The Angel of the Lord gave Gideon the instructions of how to deliver Israel from the Midianites.

Judges 13:1–5, 10–14, 21–22—An angel of the Lord promised a son to Manoah and his wife.

Daniel 3:19–26—When Shadrach, Meshach, and Abednego refused to bow to the golden image, they were thrown into a fiery furnace. When he saw a fourth man in the furnace, King Nebuchadnezzar declared that deity had joined and delivered the three Hebrew young men.

When Jesus was born in the manger at Bethlehem, He did not merely take on the form of man; He became man. It was then that God the Son became flesh. It was not enough for the Lord Jesus to visit earth for special purposes that required an appearance. He needed to become man that He might satisfy the debt of man's sin. He could not pay that debt without being the God Man. First Timothy 2:5 declares Jesus to be "the man Christ Jesus." In becoming man, He "voluntarily and gladly chose both dependence and obedience."[3] He surrendered to do the will of the Father as He left the glories of heaven to be born of lowly birth. His coming exemplifies the perfect picture of surrender. J. Oswald Sanders says, "He chose the oblivion of birth . . . humiliation of life . . . consented not only to die, but to be born."[4]

Hebrews 2:9–18 states that Jesus willingly took on the form of man and for a time was lower than the angels in order to provide the means for us to become part of His family.

Read these verses and answer the questions to understand this incredible act of love.

3. Hebrews 2:9—Why was it necessary for Jesus to be made lower than the angels for a time? _____

_____

4. Hebrews 2:10—Salvation was perfected, or complete, because Jesus was willing to do what? _____

5. Hebrews 2:14—Jesus not only died to complete salvation's plan but also destroyed what? _____

6. Hebrews 2:15—Jesus is able to free us from the slavery of what?

_____

7. Hebrews 2:17—By taking on the form of man, Jesus can understand what part of our lives? _____

_____

8. Hebrews 2:18—Why can Jesus help us when we are tempted?

_____

> Thou who art God beyond all praising,
> All for love's sake becamest Man;
> Stooping so low, but sinners raising,
> Heavenwards by Thine eternal plan.
> —*Frank Houghton*[5]

Let This Mind Be in You

Our Lord asks us to follow in His steps. He asks that we follow the example He gave us and surrender to Him as He surrendered to the will of the Father. "When we cease relating to God as our 'buddy,' as a God of convenience, and when we esteem Him in His rightful place of honor, we humbly surrender ourselves and our choices to Him."[6] His call to us is to surrender to Him as our Lord and Savior. It is easy for us to focus on ministries or occupations or projects and assure ourselves that our dedication to such activities is indeed surrender to God. But it is our lives surrendered to Him that He truly desires. When we surrender to Him, He then is able to direct our steps to whatever He will have us do. A heart fully surrendered to Him will do whatever He asks.

9. What is keeping you from total surrender to the Lord?_____

_____

10. Rank the priorities of your life and then make the list in the order that God would want them to be.

My Priorities	God's Priorities
_____ Comforts of this life	1. _____
_____ Possessions	2. _____
_____ God	3. _____
_____ Family	4. _____
_____ Occupation	5. _____
_____ Christian service	6. _____
_____ Recognition	7. _____
_____ Health	8. _____
_____ Other—	9. _____

∾ **Time to Memorize: Continue memorizing Philippians 2:5–8.**

∾ **Time for Prayer: Pray that God will give you a heart totally surrendered to Him. Ask Him to show you through this study the areas of your life that you are refusing to surrender to Him.**

> Thou who art love beyond all telling,
> Savior and King, we worship Thee!
> Immanuel, within us dwelling,
> Make us what Thou wouldst have us be.
> —*Frank Houghton*[7]

From My Heart to Yours

The matter of following God's will was just a part of my growing up. My father was a pastor of several churches in the Midwest throughout my years at home. Probably the most significant change for me came in high school. The beginning of my sophomore year in Iowa was approaching when my father was asked to candidate in a church in South Dakota. Although South Dakota was just the next state to the west, it seemed to be some isolated, desolate country to me. I addressed the opportunity with jesting. I couldn't imagine such a small town and such a small church possibly being God's will for us. I asked my dad if they had mail delivery or would an airplane drop it once a month. I wasn't being rebellious—just not serious. It was with much reluctance that I accompanied my parents and younger sister to visit this "remote" region.

To my surprise, this little town was only three miles into South Dakota. It was a nice little church with a good group of people who loved the Lord. The town was small but quaint. We visited and as we left to go home I was confident that would be my first and last visit to South Dakota. But the Lord had different plans. In the weeks that followed, both the leaders of the church and my dad felt it was God's will for him to be their pastor. I was devastated.

For the first time in my life, but not the last, I was faced with accepting the will of God that seemed to be the exact opposite of my desire. I realized I had two choices—move there with a bitter heart or move there with a heart surrendered to my parents and to God's plan for our family. I began to ask the Lord either to stop the church from officially calling my dad or to change my attitude and heart about going there. It wasn't long before I realized that God's will was for us to go to South Dakota. My heart had yielded. The adjustments weren't easy. The community was small and close-knit, which made getting to know people difficult, but in time I felt part of my new world.

Looking back over my years in South Dakota before I went to college, I recall many blessings the Lord gave me. I saw many friends from my public high school come to know the Lord. I had opportunities to minister in our church that I never would have had in a bigger setting. And I learned a lesson in surrender that I never have forgotten.

MADE IN THE LIKENESS OF MAN

Lesson 4
HIS EARLY YEARS

Philippians 2:7
But made himself of no reputation, and took upon him the
form of a servant and was made in the likeness of men.

On that first Christmas, the earthly life of the Lord Jesus began. He willingly left the splendor of heaven and came to this earth to be born in a stable in Bethlehem. The humility He showed is incomparable. He, "though rich beyond all telling, for the sake of poor sinners, became poor."[1] This miracle of Christ's birth is called the Incarnation—when God the Son took on human flesh while remaining God. He knew mankind needed what only He could provide. But to meet that need, He must be not only all God but also all man.

Jesus' Early Years

For verily he took not on him the nature of angels; but he took on him the seed of Abraham. Wherefore in all things it behoved him to be made like unto his brethren, that he might be a merciful and faithful high priest in things pertaining to God, to make reconciliation for the sins of the people. (Hebrews 2:16–17)

Jesus did not take the form of angels when He came to earth. He "took on . . . the seed of Abraham" to be "a merciful and faithful" Savior Who could understand our struggles. He grew through infancy and childhood with the same progression of development of a typical child. The difference was that Jesus' growth was not hindered by a sinful nature. His knowledge and growth came in degrees. His body and mind developed in perfect, but normal, sequence.

Jesus probably went to the synagogue training given to the boys of Nazareth. He did not receive the higher education from the rabbis in Jerusalem, yet He mastered all areas of learning. John 7:15 states that the Jews were amazed at the knowledge Jesus had. "How knoweth this man letters having never learned?" Jesus answered their questions by declaring, "My doctrine is not mine, but his that sent me" (John 7:16).

The Bible doesn't tell us much of the early life of the Lord Jesus. Mary and Joseph reared him in "Nazareth . . . a small, despised village, inhabited by a wild people."[2] Their home was filled with the traditions of the day. When Jesus was twelve years old, He went with His parents to Jerusalem to celebrate the Feast of the Passover. In fact, Jesus would have been considered a "son of the Law"[3] by this time. The next year, at age thirteen, Jesus would officially become part of the religious community. The training and teaching was already in progress to have Him ready for this important event.

∾ Time in the Word: Read Luke 2:41–52.

After you read Luke 2:41–52, answer the questions to learn of Jesus' relationship and obedience to Mary and Joseph.

1. How long did it take for them to find Him once they returned to Jerusalem?_____

2. What was Jesus doing when they found Him? _____

   _____

3. What was the response of these rabbis and teachers to Jesus' answers? _____

   _____

4. Jesus' knowledge testifies not only to His being God but also to the training He had received from Mary and Joseph. Read Deuteronomy 6:4–9. What instructions are given in these verses?

   _____

   _____

5. When Mary questioned why Jesus had stayed behind, Jesus answered her with the words "I must be about my Father's business" (verse 49). Does the "my Father" in this verse match the "thy father" in verse 48? _____

What distinction was Jesus making?_____

_____

Although Jesus was only twelve years old, He was at ease with these learned religious leaders of the temple. His understanding and answers had astonished them. Yet when He left with Mary and Joseph, He was "subject unto them" (verse 51). He was willingly obedient to them—willingly surrendered to His position as their child.

While Luke gives us only two verses that summarize how Jesus grew, we can see that His growth was typical of a young boy in a godly Jewish home. Let's compare His early development with that of Samuel and John the Baptist.

6. Read these verses and list the ways that Jesus grew and then find the description of John's and Samuel's early days.

Jesus	Luke 2:40 Luke 2:52
John the Baptist	Luke 1:66 Luke 1:80
Samuel	I Samuel 2:21 I Samuel 2:26

And Jesus increased in wisdom and stature, and in favor with God and man. (Luke 2:52)

And the spirit of the Lord shall rest upon him, the spirit of wisdom and understanding, the spirit of counsel and might, the spirit of knowledge and of the fear of the Lord; and shall make him of quick understanding in the fear of the Lord: and he shall not judge after the sight of his eyes, neither reprove after the hearing of his ears. (Isaiah 11:2–3)

LET THIS MIND BE IN YOU

7. No matter your age, you should be striving to grow in favor with God and man. Determine from Proverbs 3:1–4 what you should be doing to grow in each of these areas.

Steps from Proverbs	What I Should Be Doing
Forget not the law	
Keep the commandments	
Remember mercy and truth	
Keep truths in my heart and mind	

8. It is easy to know what we should be doing, but often much more difficult to change our actions. What things from the list above should be included in your daily schedule? List some specific personal goals for each area. _____

_____

_____

_____

_____

❧ **Time to Memorize: Continue to memorize Philippians 2:5–8.**

From My Heart to Yours

One summer when we were living in Pennsylvania, we planned a wonderful vacation with my husband's parents through New England. My daughters and I wrote letters to the tourist bureaus of the various states in the Northeast that we planned to visit. It wasn't long before we received many beautiful brochures and catalogues highlighting all the phenomenal attractions that we wouldn't want to miss. It was an exciting process putting all our ideas together. Even to this day, we all enjoy looking through the picture books of our journey.

One picture of my son, who was three at the time, always catches our eye. We were visiting the famous Concord Bridge in Massachusetts. The visitors' center had several rooms with time period furnishings. One room contained clothes that children of the day would have worn. My girls enjoyed dressing up in the historical fashions, but my son was not quite so excited about the whole process. Being the mom, I insisted he try on the appropriate costume and pose with his sisters.

It wasn't until the pictures were developed and put in the picture books that we realized the full impact of this adventure on my son. He was far from happy about the whole ordeal. Yes, he obeyed, but it was obvious that he may have looked like an eighteenth-century boy on the outside, but he was definitely a twentieth-century boy on the inside. This was not the highlight of his vacation.

This scenario never happened in the life of the Lord Jesus. He would have been obedient from the inside out. No matter the event, He would have obeyed with the spirit of surrender that God the Father desires in His children of any age. He, the One to be the perfect Savior, was also the perfect child.

His Humanity

Philippians 2:7
But made himself of no reputation, and took upon him the form of a servant, and was made in the likeness of men.

As we study Jesus' earthly ministry, we realize that He experienced and understood the trials of this life. He knew the limits of a human body and the sinless infirmities that mankind possesses. He replaced the comforts of heaven with the burdens of this world.

1. He took on the appearance of man and was recognized as just another man

   by _____ in John 14:9,

   by _____ in John 20:15, and

   by _____ in Luke 24:18.

2. He was given personal heritage through the family of _____ _____ in Romans 1:3.

3. He was described as a person made

   of _____ in Matthew 26:12,

   of _____ in Matthew 26:38,

   of _____ in Luke 23:46, and

   of _____ in Luke 24:39.

4. He also experienced certain infirmities with which we all must deal. Study the following verses and match the reference to the human infirmities Jesus knew here on this earth.

Passage		Infirmity
_____ Matthew 25:35	A.	Anger
_____ Mark 4:38	B.	Grief
_____ Luke 22:44	C.	Tiredness
_____ John 2:13–16	D.	Hunger and Thirst
_____ John 11:32–35	E.	Pain

Jesus' Baptism and Temptation

∾ **Time in the Word: Read Matthew 3:13–4:11.**

The beginning of the Lord Jesus' public ministry was a pattern of surrender. He went to the Jordan River and asked to be baptized by John the Baptist. He was obedient to God and to the plan for the ministry He was about to begin. John hesitated to grant Jesus' request because he recognized Jesus as the Son of God and realized that he was unworthy to even unlatch Jesus' sandals. John knew that Jesus, the perfect Lamb of God, did not need this act of repentance. Jesus responded to John's reluctance: "Suffer it to be so now: for thus it becometh us to fulfill all righteousness." "**Suffer it to be so** means allow it to be or let it happen. Jesus sought this outward identification with John's ministry **to fulfill all righteousness.**"[1] Jesus identified Himself with those He came to save. John and his followers witnessed God the Father giving His audible and visible blessing to Jesus with the voice from heaven and the dove resting upon Him.

Immediately after Jesus was baptized, He was led by the Holy Spirit into the wilderness to be tempted. After Jesus had fasted for forty days and nights, Satan was allowed to tempt the Lord to rebel against the will of God. This "assault of hell" occurred with the "approval of heaven."[2] The point of Satan's attack was to convince Jesus to surrender to him instead of surrendering to God. If at any point Jesus had relented to Satan's proposals, the plan of redemption would have been voided.

Jesus won a great victory not only for His role as Messiah but also for each one of us. Jesus didn't respond to the temptations with some divine, supernatural defensive tool.

5. Read the temptation of Satan and note how Jesus responded with Old Testament verses.

Verses	Temptation of Satan	Verses	Jesus' Response
Matthew 4:3		Matthew 4:4 Deuteronomy 8:3	
Matthew 4:5–6 Psalm 91:11–12		Matthew 4:7 Deuteronomy 6:16	
Matthew 4:8–9		Matthew 4:10 Deuteronomy 6:13 Deuteronomy 10:20	

Our Lord resisted Satan's attacks with the weapon of warfare He has given to each of us as believers—His Word. Oh, that we would saturate our hearts and minds with His Word so that when our times of temptation come we will be armed and ready. Without a daily time of reading, meditating on, and memorizing the Bible, we will find ourselves easily defeated by Satan's clever attacks. He knows when we are most vulnerable and won't miss the opportunity to conquer us.

We all face different kinds of temptations. What might be my greatest temptation, you might not even notice. Yet, whatever our weaknesses may be, they fall into one of the three categories of Jesus' temptations. First John 2:16 outlines these for us.

> For all that is in the world, the lust of the flesh, and the lust of the eyes, and the pride of life, is not of the Father, but is of the world.

6. Match these temptations with each category.

_____Stones into bread	A.	Lust of the Flesh
_____Angels rescue Him	B.	Lust of the Eyes
_____Rule of all the world	C.	Pride of Life

LET THIS MIND BE IN YOU

Have you ever stopped to think about the life the Lord Jesus lived while on this earth? He had a plan that was necessary for sin's debt to be paid, and the requirements to fulfill that plan were fairly simple. He had to be man. We have learned that He indeed took on the form of man. He also had to be God, and again we've seen that although He became man, He never stopped being God. He had to shed His precious blood for our sins; Hebrews 9:22b states, "Without shedding of blood there is no remission of sins."

As we look at the lifestyle of the Lord Jesus while here on the earth, we realize He could have still been our Savior and chosen to live very differently. His lifestyle and position in life were not part of His saving work. He chose a humble life, not a life of recognition and prestige. He chose a stable with a manger instead of a palace with a cradle. He chose to be born into a carpenter's family instead of the court of a king. Nazareth was His humble village instead of the glory of Jerusalem. He was raised and taught at home by Mary and Joseph instead of the instruction and care of slaves in a highly educated home. Why did He choose such hardship when luxury could have been His?

He chose to suffer the common pains of this life so that He could sympathize with us and show us the way of victory. He chose to surrender to the plan of God the Father to be able to say to us, "This is the way, walk ye in it . . ." (Isaiah 30:21b).

Hebrews 4:15 states, "For we have not an high priest which cannot be touched with the feelings of our infirmities; but was in all points tempted like as we are, yet without sin." The Lord Jesus knows our every temptation. Though He never succumbed to temptations, He lovingly and compassionately provided the victory for us by surrendering His life on the cross.

7. How do you usually handle temptations? _____

_____

8. In what areas are you struggling to have victory?_____

_____

_____

9. What promises and truths from these verses can you claim to achieve victory over these temptations?

I Corinthians 10:13 _____

_____

_____

I Corinthians 10:31 _____

_____

_____

I Corinthians 6:19_____

_____

_____

✎ **Time to Memorize: Continue to memorize Philippians 2:5–8.**

✎ **Time for Prayer: Thank the Lord Jesus for the victory over sin that you can have through Him. Thank Him for living a humble life while on this earth. He truly understands the struggles that you face.**

From My Heart to Yours

How can I stand in front of the women I teach when I am not being obedient as I should be? For the sake of my Lord, I must face my sin and with the Holy Spirit's help change.

It's easy to excuse certain sins that we can explain away or that we can put far down on our "Top Sin List." But it doesn't work that way, does it? Sin is still sin; God doesn't categorize sin in the same way we do. Why do I feel I have the privilege to think that my sin is less offensive to God? I must call my disobedience what God calls it—sin!

I could tell you the indulgence that desires to keep me defeated and depressed, but then you might use it to excuse yours. So mine shall remain, if not unnoticed, at least unacknowledged. But I told the Lord this morning that with His help it will stop having control over me. I'm ready to accept His gracious mercy. I'm ready to walk with Him in obedience in this area that "the gospel be not blamed" (Galatians 6:3). How about the sin(s) you've been condoning or explaining away? Are you ready to give them to the Lord?

He is our sympathetic Savior, our sinless example. He lived a humble, simple life on this earth that we might be confident that He understands. Go to Him now. He promises to hear and forgive. Hebrews 4:16 tells us to "come boldly unto the throne of grace, that we may obtain mercy, and find grace to help in time of need."

He alone is able to understand and help no matter what it is you face. Take time now to come boldly before Him in prayer. He will graciously hear and meet your need.

The victory is yours through Him!

MADE HIMSELF OF NO REPUTATION

A HUMBLE OCCUPATION

Philippians 2:7
But made himself of no reputation, and took upon him the form of a servant, and was made in the likeness of men.

*Ph*ilippians 2:7 shows the next aspect of the Lord Jesus' life of surrender. He "made himself of no reputation" as He ministered to the people of His day. Let's consider the words that Jesus used to describe Himself.

In Matthew 11:28–29, Jesus calls the weary to learn from Him. He declares that He is "meek and lowly in heart."

1. Consult a dictionary for the meaning of these words.

Reputation _____

Meek_____

Lowly _____

Humility _____

Notice the definitions that J. Oswald Sanders used for these words in his book *The Incomparable Christ.*[1]

Meekness—"humility in relation to God"

Lowliness—"humility in relation to man"

Sanders continues to say that "Jesus was just as meek toward God as He was lowly before man."[2] Jesus described His heart and reputation as humble and patient. His modest, submissive heart exemplifies a life surrendered in service to man for the glory of His heavenly Father. A humble occupation with a humble attitude characterized His life on this earth.

A Humble Occupation

∽ **Time in the Word: Read Mark 6:1–6.**

Is not this the carpenter, the son of Mary? (Mark 6:3)

All we know of the eighteen years from Jesus' temple visit to the beginning of His public ministry is that He worked with His earthly father as a carpenter. The people of Nazareth knew him only in this role. When He went to Nazareth to teach, the people rejected His message because they were unable to see Him as anyone except the carpenter who had grown up in their midst.

This choice of work shows us much about Jesus' humility. Through His occupation, He identified with the common man of His day and ours. He understood and honored the ordinary man. He knew the reward of working in honest labor with His hands. Those same hands that fashioned the first man and woman from the dust of the ground worked to make yokes for the oxen and furniture for the homes of His neighbors.

He no doubt worked long days, which prepared Him for the endless hours of ministry that were soon to come. His work was hidden from public eye, but all those years—six times longer than His years of ministry—were preparing Him for His purpose in coming.

In all things it behoved him to be made like unto his brethren, that he might be a merciful and faithful high priest in things pertaining to God, to make reconciliation for the sins of the people. (Hebrews 2:17)

In spite of all our modern conveniences, we seem to be rushed for time. How we often long for a few more hours in our days to complete the never-ending list of chores and duties. With each new timesaving device, our days seem to go faster without a minute to spare. What a comfort to know our Lord understands!

A Humble Attitude

2. In Philippians 2, the apostle Paul challenges Christians to follow Christ's example and humbly surrender to the will of God for their lives. To understand what characterized Christ's humility, read the following passages and note how Christ demonstrated humility.

Passage	Humility Demonstrated
Matthew 13:55	Known as the carpenter's son
Luke 22:27	
John 5:19	
John 5:30	
John 7:16	
John 8:49–50	
John 14:24	
II Corinthians 8:9	

3. God the Father rewarded Jesus' humility. Match the following verses with the outcome of His humility.

_____ Acts 2:32–36   A. Perfected or completed salvation

_____ Hebrews 1:1–2   B. Exalted by God.

_____ Hebrews 2:10   C. Made High Priest

_____ Hebrews 2:17   D. Made heir of all things

Let This Mind Be in You

The Lord Jesus not only demonstrated this grace of humility, but He also taught it. He taught it to His disciples; today He teaches us through His Word and through our circumstances. When we get a glimpse of the greatness, holiness, and righteousness of God, we are humbled.

Find what God often uses to teach us to be humble.

4. Deuteronomy 8:3—God uses _____ to humble us.

5. II Chronicles 12:5–12—God uses _____ to humble us.

6. Matthew 11:29—God uses _____ to humble us.

7. Luke 15:17–21—God uses our _____ to humble us.

8. Luke 18:13–14—God uses our _____ to humble us.

9. I Kings 3:6–11—God uses our _____ to humble us.

10. List several events in your life that God has used to humble you. From your answers for questions 4–9, decide which teaching method God used in that event.

Example: Event—Sickness of loved one

God used—Affliction

Event _____

    God used_____

Event _____

    God used_____

Event _____

    God used_____

Event _____

    God used_____

Event _____

    God used_____

11. God also rewards us as His children when we are walking with a humble attitude like that of our Lord's. Again match the verses with the outcome of our living in Christlike humility.

    _____ II Chronicles 7:14   A. Greatness

    _____ Proverbs 22:4   B. Exaltation

    _____ Isaiah 57:15   C. Blessings

    _____ Matthew 18:4   D. Grace

    _____ James 4:6   E. God's presence

    _____ James 4:10   F. Honor, riches, life

❧ **Time to Memorize: Continue memorizing Philippians 2:5–8.**

❧ **Time for Prayer: Spend time asking God to give you a humility that will glorify Him.**

From My Heart to Yours

My daughter has always loved children. When she was a little girl, she was quick to see the needs of those around her, reaching out in love and compassion. As soon as she was old enough, she helped on the bus routes of our church. She would hold the children on her lap, play with them, sing with them. She was a big sister to the little girls. Every little boy claimed her as his girlfriend. Their appearance didn't matter—soiled play-clothes, unkempt hair, sticky faces—she loved them all. When she visited their homes, she couldn't walk through their neighborhood without being greeted with squeals of delight.

So why would her dad and I be surprised to hear the excitement in her voice as she shared her new life with us!

We had helped her and her husband move to this new city, but with all the unpacking, we hadn't had the chance to look around the area. Today we had the time, and she was giving us the tour. One of the places she showed us was the local high school where she works. With her husband's responsibilities as a youth and music pastor, she is enjoying the flexible schedule of substitute teaching. She also helps with the girls' varsity volleyball team. As a volunteer, she maintains flexibility and the coaches are thrilled with the extra help. Her greatest joy is the opportunity she has to meet scores of teens that she and her husband can befriend and minister to.

She often shares the names of students for us to pray for—lives she's touching, lives she's getting to know and share. The faces are different, older than the little bus kids from the past, but her heart is unchanged as she sets aside her own comforts, loves them where they are, and introduces them to her Lord.

Lesson 7
A HUMBLE MINISTRY

Philippians 2:7
But made himself of no reputation, and took upon him the
form of a servant, and was made in the likeness of men.

*J*esus did not choose to be identified with the religious leaders of
His day, nor did the elite religious groups accept Him. He was not out
to make a name for Himself among them or to win their approval.
He ministered to the people in a quiet, simple way, not drawing attention to Himself. In fact, He rebuked the demons that identified
Him. He often told those He healed to go and tell no one Who He
was or what He had done for them.

∿ Time in the Word: Read Luke 4:31–44.

> And devils also came out of many, crying out, and saying, Thou art
> Christ the Son of God. And he rebuking them suffered them not to
> speak: for they knew that he was Christ. (Luke 4:41)

Many of Jesus' disciples and followers thought He had come to
establish an earthly kingdom and to overthrow the Roman government. Jesus had to continually remind them that His kingdom had
not yet come. On one occasion immediately after Jesus had fed a
great multitude and healed many, the people were ready to make
Him king. Jesus, aware of the people's intentions, departed alone to
pray. He understood that the plan of these enthusiastic people was
not the will of God.

Jesus experienced the demands of ministry within the limits of the sinless infirmities of His flesh. He faced the challenges of prioritizing since the demands on His time were undoubtedly endless. It was likely that the people often desired Him to keep healing and ministering when it was time to travel to the next village. How did He decide who would be the last to receive His healing touch? He had come not only to heal and restore but also to preach and teach.

A few years ago one of my sisters went on a medical mission team to Guatemala. She worked with an oral surgeon to help meet the dental needs of the people in the small village. Long lines of people met them—people who had walked many miles from the neighboring towns and villages. The lines of needy people seemed to never end; each day brought more faces and more needs. The day would end with the line as long as it had been when the day began. The long days of service seemed only to scratch the surface of the medical needs of these Guatemalans.

I can imagine that the lines to see Jesus were not much different from these lines in a modern-day Third-World country. His reputation for caring and healing would have quickly traveled the Palestinian countryside just as the news of my sister's medical mission team spread through this area of Guatemala. How do we keep our focus as we minister to others? The tasks at times seem overwhelming. We must continually evaluate our purpose and motives.

Jesus ministered to the people where He found them. He practiced a personal approach to ministry. He had compassion for the multitudes and time for the individual. He didn't expect the people to come to Him; He went to them. He could have met the needs of multitudes with only one thought or one word, but He chose to touch them each as individuals with individual needs. He also could have ministered only to those who approached Him or those who participated in the scheduled worship times of the synagogue. Instead Jesus met people where they were and often initiated their encounter.

1. Read the following passages and note the person Jesus ministered to and where they were when they met the Savior.

Passage	Person(s)	Where were they?	What were they doing?
Matthew 4:18–20	Peter and Andrew	By the sea	Fishing in the Sea of Galilee
Matthew 4:21–22			
Matthew 9:9			
Matthew 9:10–13			
Luke 4:38–44			
Luke 10:38–42			
Luke 19:2–10			

LET THIS MIND BE IN YOU

Jesus' approach has not changed. He still comes to each of us where we are and loves us just as we are. He doesn't ask us to change our lives or hearts and then come to Him. He desires for us to come to Him and let Him save us. Then He changes us through His mercy and grace. He personally invites each of us to come to Him.

And the Spirit and the bride say, Come, And let him that heareth say, Come. And let him that is athirst come. And whosoever will, let him take the water of life freely. (Revelation 22:17)

Read the following verses to see what precious promises He gives us when we come to Him.

2. Matthew 11:28–30 _____

3. John 3:15–16 _____

4. John 6:37 _____

5. Romans 10:13 _____

> Hereby perceive we the love of God, because he laid down his life for us: and we ought to lay down our lives for the brethren. But whoso hath this world's good, and seeth his brother have need, and shutteth up his bowels of compassion from him, how dwelleth the love of God in him? My little children, let us not love in word, neither in tongue; but in deed and in truth. (I John 3:16–18)

Jesus wants me to love people where they are.

When we realize all our Lord has done for us, our hearts should be ready to reach out to those around us with the same loving, humble approach. He does not want us to partake in the sins of those around us to gain opportunity to minister to them, but He does ask that we love them and minister to them with the same heart that He has for them. "The standard for our love is God's love in Christ, who died for us. Love that observes need, and does not act to minister to it, is no love at all."[1]

6. Would you describe your love for others as Christlike? Is your daily walk characterized by humility and compassion?_____

We must never forget where we were when we realized Jesus' love for us. We were no more deserving of His love than any of those He touched while here on this earth. He lovingly gives us salvation as we call on His name. He graciously sustains us as we walk through this life. He compassionately carries every burden we lay at His feet. Yet we have not earned these privileges. When we get a glimpse of what He does for us on a daily basis, our hearts should overflow with a gratitude that we cannot help but share with those around us. We should strive daily to reach out to anyone anywhere to show them the love of our Lord and Savior.

Answer the following questions based on the verses given and be reminded of our responsibility to minister to others.

7. II Corinthians 5:14—What should be my motivation as I minister to those around me?_____

8. Galatians 2:20—What part should my own desires have as I follow Christ? _____

9. James 1:22–27—What two kinds of Christians are described here?_____

   Describe each. _____

   _____

10. What are the two tests of "pure religion" according to James 1:27?

    a. _____

    b. _____

11. Based on these verses from James, how would you describe your service for the Lord? Are you a hearer or a doer? _____

12. How do your efforts measure up to the tests of true religion?

    _____

    _____

    _____

෴ Time to Memorize: Continue to memorize Philippians 2:5–8.

෴ Time for Prayer: Ask the Lord to make you a humble servant to those who come across your path today.

Come, Ye Sinners, Poor and Needy
Come, ye weary, heavy laden,
Lost and ruined by the fall;
If you tarry till you're better,
You will never come at all.

Let not conscience make you linger,
Nor of fitness fondly dream;
All the fitness He requireth
Is to feel your need of Him.

I will arise and go to Jesus,
He will embrace me in His arms;
In the arms of my dear Savior,
O there are ten thousand charms.

—*Joseph Hart*[2]

From My Heart to Yours

The call had come late on a Sunday night. It was a nurse from the emergency room of a nearby hospital. The teenage girl who requested that my husband and I be called was a student in our Christian school and attended our church. Just a few hours before, she had taken an undetermined number of pills in an attempt to end her life.

When we arrived, we were taken to the room where she was being treated. Her father and mother stood off to the side. It was evident that her parents were not able to deal with what was happening in front of them. Their years of drug and alcohol abuse had left them at a loss as to how to help their struggling daughter.

We hadn't been in the room long before I was by the girl's side holding her and comforting her as she vomited the remaining drugs and charcoal. After each purging, it would take several minutes to get her cleaned up and comfortable before the process would repeat itself. As a mother of three, I marveled at this forlorn, confused woman who stood watching me care for her daughter. Before we left, I tried to engage the mother's help in this gruesome but necessary process.

Was I a hero for helping in a role that shouldn't have been necessary with the girl's parents so close by? No. I was simply meeting this girl where she was that night—in spite of the hours of past counsel that should have prevented such an occasion. I met her in an attempt to show her a God Who loved her even where she was.

What limits do you place on your service to others? Is your reputation within your community or church more important to you than the needs of the humblest around you? How far will you extend yourself beyond convenience and comfort to meet the spiritual and physical needs of the lives the Lord has called you to touch?

TOOK UPON HIM THE FORM OF A SERVANT

Lesson 8
A Servant's Heart

Philippians 2:7
**But made himself of no reputation, and took upon him the
form of a servant, and was made in the likeness of men.**

*I*n the past year I have done some substitute teaching in a local
Christian school. Although I had taught third grade years ago, I was
amazed that many things about them remain unchanged. One of
the big consistencies was in the role of leadership. To the average
third grader being line leader is still a position of great significance.
Something about being first in line gives a child a feeling of accom-
plishment. (I guess I still feel that way as I occasionally am first in a
checkout line that just opened.) This coveted position is a place of
prestige and importance not to be taken lightly.

Something within each of us constantly tempts us to fight for our
rights and privileges. We desire to be recognized and served in ways
that pamper our egos and feed our self-awareness. Yet, as we consider the life of the Lord Jesus, we realize that His interaction with
the people around Him was in direct opposition to this self-centered
philosophy. In His coming to earth, He not only laid aside all position and honor but also became a man of self-sacrificing service. Let's
study some passages to see how His approach to service manifested
itself.

As a Little Child

On several occasions Jesus taught His disciples the meaning of service. He continually had to refocus the disciples' attentions, as they were prone to desire the status and recognition as the "Best Disciple" or "Most Likely to Succeed."

His twelve closest followers often argued among themselves about who was worthy of the positions closest to Jesus. Jesus used these occasions to challenge them to have His heart—the heart of a servant.

Read Mark 9:30–37, focusing on how Jesus instructed the disciples in the area of service.

1. Jesus told His disciples about what three events (vv. 30–31)?

   _____

   _____

2. What was their response (v. 32)? _____

   _____

3. What was their focus while Jesus was teaching (vv. 33–34)?

   _____

4. Did Jesus know what was going on between the disciples (v. 35)?

   _____

5. When Jesus gathered the disciples around Him, what did He teach them about His definition of greatness (v. 35)? _____

   _____

6. Who did He use to illustrate His teaching (vv. 36–37)? _____

7. What truth did He teach the disciples with this illustration?

   _____

   _____

8. According to Mark 9:35, if someone wants to be first, she must be
_____ and _____

As He That Serveth

☙ **Time in the Word: Read Mark 10:32–45.**

In Mark 10:32–34, Jesus spoke again to His disciples about the events that were soon to come. He wanted them to be ready for the unfolding of redemption's plan, yet the disciples seemed to find the predictions of the coming days unsettling. They struggled for some definite security for their futures. Two brothers, James and John, asked Jesus for special positions in His future glory. They wanted to sit one on His right hand and the other on His left. According to Matthew 20:20–21, they even had their mother, Salome, ask the Lord for these special seats of honor.

Look again at the passage in Mark and consider the response these brothers received from Jesus and the other disciples.

9. When the other ten disciples heard what James and John were asking, they were _____ (Mark 10:41).

10. Jesus again gathered the disciples around Him. He said they were acting like the _____ (Mark 10:42).

11. Their response was completely opposite of what Jesus wanted. According to Mark 10:43–44, to be great is to _____; and to be first means you will be _____

12. Jesus' purpose for coming was not to be _____, but to _____ and give His _____ a ransom for many (Mark 10:45).

Another passage in Luke tells of the Lord Jesus' challenge to His disciples in this area of service. Again there was a rivalry among the disciples about who should be considered great.

> And there was also a strife among them, which of them should be accounted the greatest. And he said unto them, The kings of the Gentiles exercise lordship over them; and they that exercise authority

upon them are called benefactors. But ye shall not be so: but he that is greatest among you, let him be as the younger; and he that is chief, as he that doth serve. For whether is greater, he that sitteth at meat, or he that serveth? is not he that sitteth at meat? but I am among you as he that serveth. (Luke 22:24–27)

The Gentile kings would "rule with an iron hand, and then take a title that extolled their benevolence."[1] Jesus told His followers that they should do neither. He declared that the one who is greatest is the one who considers himself as the younger, and the one who is the leader is the one who serves others. To illustrate His point even further, Jesus used a common scenario of their day. He asked who is greater—the one at the table to be served or the one serving? He answered His own question—the one being served. Then He proclaimed His surrendered heart—

I am among you as he that serves.

As an Attitude of His Heart

Jesus was humble and submissive to the will of the Father. He had not come to be exalted as King at this time. He came with the attitude of a perfect servant to minister to a lost and dying world. His love for mankind was not disingenuous but saturated with a godly love for lost mankind. He came as Savior knowing He would return as Lord and King.

13. Read the following verses and match them to the phrases that describe His attitude.

_____ Isaiah 53:7	A. Meek and lowly
_____ Zechariah 9:9	B. Became poor
_____ Matthew 11:29	C. Straitened or distressed
_____ Luke 12:50	D. Sought the will of the Father
_____ John 5:30	E. Just and lowly
_____ II Corinthians 8:9	F. No reputation, servant
_____ Philippians 2:7	G. Sheep before shearers

Let This Mind Be in You

In John 17:4, Jesus declares to God the Father, "I have glorified thee on the earth: I have finished the work which thou gavest me to do." Oh, that those same words could be ours as we one day stand in His presence!

14. Evaluate your service to God by answering the following questions based on the truths of the various verses.

    WHEN may I want to quit?

    Proverbs 24:10 _____

    WHY may I want to quit?

    Proverbs 24:10 _____

    HOW should I want to be found?

    I Corinthians 4:2 _____

    WHO is faithful to me as I serve?

    I Thessalonians 5:24 _____

    WHAT has God given me?

    II Timothy 1:7 _____

ᔆ **Time to Memorize: Continue to memorize Philippians 2:5–8.**

ᔆ **Time for Prayer: Ask God to show you any areas of service that you are not doing with the heart of a servant.**

From My Heart to Yours

At times we each must ask ourselves some tough questions. It's not always easy to be honest when it comes to evaluating our own motives. How would you describe your heart for service? Would you have been in the middle of the disciples' arguing for your deserved place beside Jesus? We all know the answers we are supposed to give when these tough questions are asked. But I challenge you to look closely at your heart as you answer the list of questions below. How should you honestly answer them?

Am I hurt when people don't acknowledge what I've done?_____

Am I not interested in helping if I have to work under someone else's leadership? _____

Do I want to share the task or ministry with anyone else? _____

Do I get irritated when someone else is asked to do something that I feel I can do better? _____

Do I hesitate to take a task if no one will know that I'm the one who did it? _____

Carefully consider the words of the following poem. May it be the prayer of your heart today!

Servant's Heart
Make me a servant like You, dear Lord,
Living for others each day:
Humble and meek, helping the weak,
Loving in all that I say.

Make me a witness like You, dear Lord,
Showing the love of the cross—
Sharing Your Word till all have heard,
Serving whatever the cost.

Give me, Lord, a servant's heart.
Here's my life; take ev'ry part.
Give me, Lord, a servant's heart.
Help me draw so close to You
That Your love comes shining through.
Give me, Lord, a servant's heart.
Give me, Lord, a servant's heart.

—*Ron Hamilton*[2]

Lesson 9
A Servant's Actions

Philippians 2:7
But made himself of no reputation, and took upon him the form of a servant, and was made in the likeness of men.

Jesus' ministry was characterized with His good and gracious acts of kindness. Acts 10:38 states, "God anointed Jesus of Nazareth with the Holy Ghost and with power: who went about doing good, and healing all that were oppressed of the devil; for God was with him." No event in the life of the Lord Jesus shows His servant's heart better than the night in the upper room after He and the disciples celebrated the Passover feast. Only John's Gospel gives us this insightful account. The disciples and Jesus had just finished eating the Passover supper, and Judas's scheme of betrayal was already planned. Jesus took a moment and pondered Who He was.

Jesus knowing that the Father had given all things into his hands, and that He was come from God, and went to God. (John 13:3)

Jesus clearly knew Who He was. He knew His majesty and glory. He knew He was about to fulfill the plan of redemption. He knew that God the Father had placed within His view the power to forgive all mankind of their sins. He knew that as He had come from heaven very soon He would return to His heavenly home. He was vividly aware of all the glory due Him. And with those thoughts of splendor, He rose from the table.

He could have shown His majesty to His closest friends in an unprecedented way. He could have demanded they bow before Him in humble submission as their Creator. He could have declared Himself to be their Prophet, Priest, and King. But that was not what He did.

Instead, He removed His outer garments, filled a basin with water, took a towel, and began the most menial, humble task usually reserved for the lowliest of servants. He began to wash the feet of the disciples. One by one He washed and dried each disciple's feet. "Perhaps Jesus had waited for one of the disciples to perform this task, but they were evidently debating who should be the greatest."[1] The account of the disciples' rivalry in Luke 22:24–27, which we studied in Lesson 8, takes place during this special meal together. When the apostles failed to carry out this customary practice, Jesus gave them an unforgettable portrait of a servant's heart.

Time in the Word: Read John 13:1–17.

1. What was Peter's response to Jesus' actions (John 13:6–10)? _____

_____

_____

2. Why did Jesus wash His disciples' feet (John 13:12–15)? _____

_____

3. What lesson did He want them to learn? _____

4. What did Jesus say would be the result of knowing and doing these things (John 13:17)? _____

A Servant's Example

For even hereunto were ye called: because Christ also suffered for us, leaving us an example, that ye should follow his steps. (I Peter 2:21)

When Jesus rose from the table at the end of the meal, He gave a vivid picture of the example He wanted all believers to follow. "If humility was the distinguishing feature of the Master, then it must characterize the disciple. He was not only a standing rebuke to pride, but a living example of humility."[2] The apostles and other inspired writers of the New Testament were very much aware of their responsibility to follow Christ and have the heart of a servant. Oh, that we each would follow the example He sets for us in John 13!

5. Read the opening verses of these New Testament books and note the introductory words the Holy Spirit directed these men to use.

Passage	Inspired Writer	Description of Writer
Romans 1:1	Paul	Servant of Jesus Christ
James 1:1		
II Peter 1:1		
Jude 1		
Revelation 1:1		

6. Study the following passages and note what God's Word teaches about being a servant.

Passage	Servant's Heart
Mark 9:35	Servant to all, first shall be last
Mark 10:43–45	
Luke 17:10	
I Corinthians 7:21–24	
Galatians 5:13	

Let This Mind Be in You

We as believers are to be like our Lord Jesus Christ and follow in His footsteps. The first way we should demonstrate a servant's heart is in our service to Him. A word often used in the Bible for servant means bondslave. A bondslave is "one who has chosen to be the servant of another willingly and has an undying and complete loyalty. The will of the master is paramount in this servant's life. This is the servant we are to be to Jesus."[3] We need to approach our service to the Lord Jesus in this way. Our service should be from a heart of devotion and love, willingly suffering and sacrificing our all for Him. We need a heart that is surrendered totally in service to Him.

What do the following verses teach about our service to our Lord?

> If any man serve me, let him follow me; and where I am, there shall also my servant be: if any man serve me, him will my Father honour. (John 12:26)

7. To serve the Lord we must also do what?_____

8. What does God the Father do to the one who faithfully follows the Lord Jesus?_____

> Knowing this, that our old man is crucified with him, that the body of sin might be destroyed, that henceforth we should not serve sin. (Romans 6:6)

9. Because of what Jesus accomplished on the cross, He gives us the power to serve Him and not to _____

> And whatsoever ye do, do it heartily, as to the Lord, and not unto men; knowing that of the Lord ye shall receive the reward of the inheritance: for ye serve the Lord Christ. (Colossians 3:23–24)

10. How should our service be done? _____

11. Whatever our task, we are ultimately serving whom?_____

_____

In reality, our service to Jesus is done through our serving others. We may find our "others" to be our employer, our government, or our families; yet in our service to these people, we are ministering to our Lord Jesus. Our actions and attitudes toward those around us are indicators of our heart toward Him.

Read Matthew 25:34–46.

12. Matthew 25:35–36; 42–44—What did Jesus say these people had or had not given to Him?

    a. _____

    b. _____

    c. _____

    d. _____

    e. _____

    f. _____

13. Matthew 25:37–39—Did they realize their actions involved Him? _____

14. Matthew 25:40—What was the explanation for the credit they received? _____

_____

15. Matthew 25:34—What inheritance was given to those who had done these things? _____

16. Matthew 25:41, 46—What were they given for not doing these things? _____

17. What are you doing to serve those around you? _____

_____

_____

18. Do you do those things as unto the Lord, or do you do them with a heart of resentment and impatience? _____

⚘ **Time to Memorize: Continue to memorize Philippians 2:5–8.**

❧ **Time for Prayer: Spend time asking the Lord to help you have a heart to serve Him as you serve those around you.**

From My Heart to Yours

Long before the days of minivans and SUVs, a family that included more than two offspring faced a dilemma every time they needed to go somewhere—who would sit in the middle of the back seat! I realize this will date me, but those from my generation will no doubt remember this well. For those of you without that distant memory, let me explain. The cars in those days had a rounded protrusion in the floor of the back seat. Something to do with the axles, wheels, or tires was the answer I was given when I regularly inquired about this seemingly purposeless shape to the floorboard. Although this projection was harmless in itself, it was horribly inconvenient to the one sitting in the middle rear seat. Hence, the problem among siblings. Who would be the one to sit there with knees nearly above one's head? As the third daughter of four I seemed to be destined to this spot. My younger sister naturally would get the spot in the front with Dad and Mom. My two older sisters would pull the age issues out and proceed with a defense of their right to have the window seats. That left me—in the middle in more ways than one. Even the smallest of joy rides were quickly dampened with the discussion of seating arrangements. Such occasions in families all across our country no doubt led to the design of the modern vehicles that comfortably seat more than four.

I can only imagine that the disciples and my sisters and I sounded similar as we struggled for our self-declared rightful place. The Lord Jesus exemplifies for us a different approach to life—servant leadership. Our battles change specifics as we age, but if we look carefully, we soon realize that we still want our own way. Our focus is self-centered instead of others-centered. Oh, that we would set ourselves aside and lovingly serve our families, our friends, our neighbors with a heart like His.

OBEDIENT UNTO DEATH

Lesson 10
THE SURRENDER OF THE SON

Philippians 2:8
**And being found in fashion as a man, he humbled himself, and
became obedient unto death, even the death of the cross.**

Our last lesson ended with the Lord Jesus washing the feet of His
disciples. He gave us a beautiful picture of a servant-leader. He de-
picted the perfect example of the servant's heart that He had taught
throughout His three-year ministry. When He and His disciples had
finished the Passover feast, they ended their special observance together with the singing of a hymn.

> And when they had sung an hymn, they went out into the mount of
> Olives. (Matthew 26:30)

The songs that were sung were taken from Psalm 115–118. These
psalms were called "the Hallel (praise) Psalms."[1] They take on a special meaning as we consider the events soon to follow. Only Jesus
could foresee what lay ahead. The disciples did not comprehend
what Jesus had warned them about many times. The plan of salvation would "unfold like a book already written . . . penned before the
foundation of the world."[2]

Read these verses from Psalms, which Jesus and His disciples possibly sang. Reflect on their meaning as you study these lessons about
Jesus' surrender to the death He was soon to face.

> What shall I render unto the Lord for all his benefits toward me? I
> will take the cup of salvation, and call upon the name of the Lord. I

will pay my vows unto the Lord now in the presence of all his people. (Psalm 116:12–14)

The Lord is on my side; I will not fear: what can man do unto me? The Lord taketh my part with them that help me: therefore shall I see my desire upon them that hate me. (Psalm 118:6–7)

The stone which the builders refused is become the head stone of the corner. This is the Lord's doing; it is marvellous in our eyes. This is the day which the Lord hath made; we will rejoice and be glad in it. (Psalm 118:22–24)

The Garden of Gethsemane

After the final hymn of the Passover was sung, Jesus took His disciples to a meaningful place. He had often come to this special spot when He needed time away from the demands of the multitudes. He came here for solitude to spend time in prayer with the Father. He knew the importance of stepping aside from the demands of life to spend quiet time and be refreshed from the demands of this world through fellowship with His heavenly Father.

Read the following passages and note what took place in Jesus' life just before and just after He took time alone with the Father. Also notice where He chose to go for this time of solitude.

1. Matthew 14:1–13

   Before _____

   Where _____

   After _____

2. Matthew 14: 21–25

   Before _____

   Where _____

   After _____

3. Mark 1:34–39

Before _____

Where _____

After _____

4. Luke 6:10–13

Before _____

Where _____

After _____

5. Luke 9:1–2, 11

Before _____

Where _____

After _____

6. Luke 9:23–29

Before _____

Where _____

After _____

7. John 6:15–21

Before _____

Where _____

After _____

8. John 10:39–42

Before _____

Where _____

After _____

Jesus' times of solitude came between significant times of ministry. To be ready for what was coming, He made sure He had the time to be refreshed from His ministry. If the Lord Jesus needed times apart, how much more do you and I need times of refreshing alone with our heavenly Father!

The disciples were probably not surprised to realize the Garden of Gethsemane was their destination that night. Luke 22:39 says, "And he came out, and went as he was wont [accustomed], to the mount of Olives; and his disciples also followed him." He "evidently . . . had been making it a habit in the closing week to withdraw for prayer."[3]

Surrender to the Will of the Father

∽ **Time in the Word: Read Matthew 26:36–46.**

Answer the questions to be reminded of what took place in this garden spot on this historic night.

9. What instructions did Jesus give to the disciples in verse 36?

_____

10. Jesus took Peter, James, and John with Him farther into the garden. What did He ask His closest disciples to do (vv. 37–38)?

_____

_____

11. How many times did Jesus find these disciples sleeping? _____

12. Why did Jesus want the disciples to pray (v. 41)?_____

_____

13. What did Jesus ask His Father to do (v. 42)? _____

_____

14. How do we know that Jesus was submissive to the desires of God the Father (v. 42)?_____

_____

15. How many times did Jesus pray this prayer?_____

Before we consider the request that Jesus made to God the Father, let's look at what the Lord Jesus endured as He prayed. His suffering was intense as He faced the mission that lay before Him. Any hardship or suffering He had endured up to this time was minor compared to what He was about to face. He became extremely distraught as He realized the coming agony. In an earlier passage Satan tempted Him in the wilderness with the attraction of glory and gratification. Now Satan attempted to overwhelm Him with the anticipation of the extreme suffering He would soon face. Satan hoped Jesus would abandon the plan of redemption to avoid this intense agony.[4]

16. Read each passage and note the phrases that describe what Jesus experienced.

Passage	His Response
Matthew 26:37	
Matthew 26:38	
Mark 14:33	
Luke 22:44	

"Abba, Father"

And he said, Abba, Father, all things are possible unto thee; take away this cup from me: nevertheless not what I will, but what thou wilt. (Mark 14:36)

The first thing we want to consider is the name Jesus used as He addressed God the Father. He called Him "Abba"—the Aramaic word for "Father."[5] Abba is similar to our "Daddy" or "Papa."[6] I was twenty-five years old when my father went to be with the Lord. He

55. Our relationship had been a very special one. I would watch him by the hour while he built things for our home and be his helper, handing him the tools he needed. I can still imagine him reading in his favorite chair. He was not only my father but also my pastor for all but a few of those years that we shared. I learned much about God's Word as I attended classes he taught and church services he preached. He answered many of my spiritual questions as I leaned up from the back seat of our car on the ride home from church. Although I went away to college, married, and began my own family, he was always my "daddy." Time couldn't change that relationship and neither could his death.

This term expressed the precious relationship of a child to his father, but it was never used to describe a man's relationship to God. Jesus' use of the name "Abba" pictures for us His "unique relationship to God."[7] As He knelt there in the garden, He needed the comfort of His heavenly Father as He faced death.

Let This Mind Be in You

There are only two other times this name "Abba" is used in Scripture. Read these verses to see how this intimate family term was used.

17. Romans 8:14–17—How does the believer become a child in the family of God? _____

_____

How does this term picture our relationship to God?_____

_____

18. Galatians 4:3–7—How does this name for God show the contrast of our past and current relationship to God? _____

_____

Who helps us to realize our new relationship to God as our Father? _____

19. In order to maintain a close relationship with anyone, you must spend time with him or her. What are you doing daily to nurture your relationship with your heavenly Father? _____

_____

20. Can you honestly call God "Abba"?_____

21. What do you need to do or change to have this kind of relationship with God?_____

_____

✎ **Time to Memorize: Continue to memorize Philippians 2:5–8.**

✎ **Time for Prayer: Spend time today confessing any sin that may be hindering your relationship to God. Ask God to show you the areas of your life that you still have not surrendered to Him.**

From My Heart to Yours

No matter what your relationship is with your earthly father, you can know the love and care of your heavenly Father. Through His Word we can learn of Him and grow in our knowledge of Him. And with that knowledge comes greater dependence and trust. Surrender your heart and life to Him today. He eagerly awaits your decision to have this close loving relationship with Him.

Abba, Father
Father, hold me safe in Your arms;
Father, keep me free from all harm.
I cast my care on You
Just like a child should do—
Trusting, loving all that You are.

Father, help me lean on You more
Through each valley, through ev'ry storm.
Help me when I can't see
Your will is best for me;
Love me, hold me sheltered and warm.

Father, mold me, make me like new.
Guide my footsteps, keep my heart true—
So that the world may see
Your likeness lives in me.
Break me, shape me, make me like You.

Abba, Father, I rest in you;
You're always faithful,
You're always true.
Abba, Father, You are my song
Though clouds are dark,
Though night is long.
I cry to You, Abba, Father.

—*Ron Hamilton*[8]

Lesson 11
THE SURRENDER IN PRAYER

Philippians 2:8
And being found in fashion as a man, he humbled himself, and became obedient unto death, even the death of the cross.

*I*n our last lesson we looked at the events of the Garden of Gethsemane with Jesus and His disciples. Let's continue our look at what took place that night in the garden to better understand what the cost of surrender was to the Lord Jesus. As He agonized over what lay ahead, He faced some crucial decisions that night. If we look at His prayer, phrase by phrase, we get a better idea of what Jesus suffered that night.

❧ Time in the Word: Read Mark 14:32–42.

"All things are possible unto thee"—Jesus acknowledged that God can do all things. Nothing is beyond His reach or power. God Himself had planned the course of mankind's salvation and only He could alter those plans. Jesus gave God the Father the glory that only He can claim. The plan He had chosen for man's salvation was about to be completed.

"Take away this cup from me"—Jesus was not afraid of what lay before Him. He knew that in bearing the sins of all mankind He would experience the "wrath of God . . . the divine wrath . . . as man's sin-bearer."[1] Jesus knew His Father would turn away His face from Him as He bore all the past, present, and future sins of the entire world.

"The full throttle of divine impact and emotion was almost more than one human body could endure."[2] Satan bombarded Christ with all his forces in an attempt to stop the work of the Cross.

"Nevertheless not what I will, but what thou wilt"—The Lord Jesus set aside all the attacks of Satan and surrendered to the will of God the Father. In human form, He, with fear and anguish, anticipated what was to come. But as God, He willingly submitted to the Father for the salvation plan to be accomplished through His death and resurrection. In Hebrews 5:7–9, we see that God's plan was necessary for the salvation of sinful man to be accomplished. Through the obedience of the Lord Jesus, we can know His saving grace.

> Who in the days of his flesh, when he had offered up prayers and supplications with strong crying and tears unto him that was able to save him from death, and was heard in that he feared; though he were a Son, yet learned he obedience by the things which he suffered; and being made perfect, he became the author of eternal salvation unto all them that obey him. (Hebrews 5:7–9)

Through Jesus' willingness to die He gave us the perfect illustration of obedience to God's will. Read the following passages to see what is involved with being surrendered to the will of God.

1. Deuteronomy 11:13—We are to love and serve the Lord with all our _____ and with all our _____

2. Deuteronomy 28:14—We are to obey God's will without getting

   _____

3. Joshua 22:2—We are to obey _____ God's will for us.

4. Psalm 119:35—We are to obey God's will with _____

5. Psalm 143:10—We must ask God to _____ us His will.

6. Isaiah 1:19—We must be _____ and obedient to receive the blessings God has intended for us.

7. Isaiah 1:20—If we refuse to obey God's will, we can expect

   _____

8. Jeremiah 7:23—If we obey God's voice, we will be His _____ and it will be _____ with us.

9. James 1:25—If we do the work God has called us to, we will be _____ by God.

Many Bible characters illustrate man's struggle to obey God's will. Those who willingly obeyed found the results to be blessing. Those who refused to obey God's will suffered in some way.

10. Read the following verses and fill in the chart. Note who obeyed or disobeyed and the results of their decisions.

Disobedience and the Results	Passage	Obedience and the Results
Adam and Eve had to leave the Garden/Sin entered the world	Genesis 3:6, 11, 24	
	Genesis 6:22	
	Numbers 20:8–12	
	Numbers 32:11–12	
	I Samuel 28:17	
	I Kings 17:5–6	

I'm so glad that God inspired the writers of Scripture to include this verse: "There appeared an angel unto him from heaven, strengthening him" (Luke 22:43). When the night of struggle had reached the point of full surrender, God sent this messenger from heaven to strengthen the Lord Jesus.

Let This Mind Be in You

Many times we too must agonize over whether to obey God. The battle can be long and lonely, yet we can be assured that God will not give us more than we can endure. He will send to us the encouragement we need as we faithfully surrender to His will for our lives. God gives to us His grace, His enabling power, to remain steadfast as we face times of temptation, trial, decision, and surrender. What a blessed hope!

11. The following exercise gives us insight into God's provision of endurance and man's display of that provision. Read the verses and match the reference with the word that will finish the sentence.

God _____ my endurance to walk in obedience to His will for me.

_____ Psalm 16:8   A. provides for
_____ Psalm 55:22   B. exemplifies
_____ Philippians 4:1   C. maintains
_____ James 1:17   D. commands

My endurance to walk in His will for me will be seen in my _____ God.

_____ I Corinthians 15:58   A. faith in
_____ Hebrew 3:6   B. hope in
_____ Hebrews 10:23   C. work for
_____ Colossians 2:5   D. rejoicing in

12. What areas of your life do you need to surrender to the Lord?

_____

_____

13. In what areas of your life have you been tempted to do things your way instead of God's way?_____

_____

_____

ᔕ **Time to Memorize: Continue to memorize Philippians 2:5–8.**

ᔕ **Time for Prayer: Ask God to forgive you for the times you have set aside His will to do your own. Ask Him to show you other areas that you need to surrender completely to Him.**

From My Heart to Yours

Our farmhouse sat on one of the highest spots in our little mountain town on the edge of the Pocono Mountains of Pennsylvania. We were just a half-mile from a game preserve, and the wide-open backyard eventually met a line of trees, but not too soon to make flying kites difficult. My girls were two and four years old when we moved there, and our son was born within our first years. My husband pastored a small Baptist church that was filled with wonderful people—many of whom were old enough to be our parents. They warmly welcomed my husband and me, and our children soon became adopted grandchildren to many. When they would baby-sit for us, these precious adopted grandmas would come in pairs to share in the fun. Our life was quiet for the most part, and the struggles we had were mostly personal as the Lord worked on us to make us better vessels for His service.

But the day came that the Lord saw fit to call us to a different ministry. We were in the beginning stages of some expansion plans for our ministry when the Lord began to lay on my husband's heart a call to change. We sought God's will for us as a family. We saw God open the doors and unmistakably guide our steps to a new ministry as different from our mountaintop refuge as it could be.

Our quiet ministry was replaced with a ministry of trials. The years that followed were filled with many challenges. Our strength and wisdom were stretched beyond what we thought possible. We were physically and emotionally extended beyond what we thought we could endure. Yet God was faithful. He reminded us often that His will had led us there and His grace would sustain us.

God's will is not always the easiest path from our perspective. But His example in the Garden of Gethsemane shows us that He understands our struggles. He, as God, faced the hours ahead with full knowledge of all He would endure; yet, He willingly surrendered to the will of God the Father. He would fulfill redemption's plan—no matter the cost. How can I do less than unreservedly surrender my life to His will for me! May we daily say with our Lord, "Not my will, but Thine be done!"

MY LIFE SURRENDERED

Lesson 12
MY LIFE SURRENDERED

Romans 12:1

I beseech you therefore, brethren, by the mercies of God, that ye present your bodies a living sacrifice, holy, acceptable unto God, which is your reasonable service.

As we bring our study to a close, we need to apply what we have learned. Ask yourself, "Am I daily surrendering my life to God?" By taking a close look at the life of the Lord Jesus, we have seen how He lived totally surrendered to the will of the Father. We have been challenged to evaluate each aspect of our lives as we have studied His. But it's not enough to know about surrender. It's not enough to understand its meaning. It's not even enough to understand that the Lord Jesus is our perfect Example. This biblical surrender demands a daily commitment to present our bodies, our lives, as living sacrifices for His service. We are required to respond with action. We must be motivated by a heart that has set self aside; the Lord Jesus must be given our full obedience and worship. In this last lesson consider whether your life is truly consecrated to Him.

Many characters throughout the Bible picture the desire and struggle of trying to live submitted to God. When we look at the accounts of their lives, we see that this surrender must be day by day, moment by moment. From their lives we can learn that this life is possible in any circumstance if we are relying on God's grace. Join me now as we take a close look at several Bible characters who illustrate this for us.

Read the following passages and fill in the details of the lives of these people from the Bible. Notice the people, their situation, God's will, and the outcome of their following God's will.

1. Genesis 6:5–8, 13–14; 7:1–5; 8:1–5

   Person _____

   Situation _____

   _____

   God's will _____

   Choice _____

   Outcome_____

2. Numbers 13:1–3, 26–33; 14:6–9, 34–38; Joshua 14:6–10

   Persons _____

   Situation _____

   _____

   God's will _____

   Choice _____

   Outcome_____

3. Daniel 3:12, 8–30; Exodus 20:3–4

   Persons _____

   Situation _____

   _____

   God's will _____

   Choice _____

   Outcome_____

4. Daniel 6:1–23; Exodus 20:4

Person _____

Situation _____

_____

God's will _____

Choice _____

Outcome _____

5. Now read the following verses to find the different areas of our lives we are to surrender to God's will and control. Match the verse with what God wants us to willingly give to Him.

_____ Joshua 24:15   A. Words and meditations of the heart

_____ Psalm 19:14   B. Money

_____ Psalm 37:4   C. Service and family

_____ Proverbs 3:26   D. Bodies

_____ Proverbs 23:26   E. Time

_____ Isaiah 26:3   F. Future

_____ Romans 12:1   G. Heart

_____ II Corinthians 9:7   H. Delights

_____ Ephesians 5:16   I. Mind

_____ James 4:14   J. Confidence

Let This Mind Be in You

Time in the Word: Read Philippians 2:5–11.

6. What have you learned from the life of the Lord Jesus and His surrender? As you consider each phrase of Philippians 2:5–8, remind yourself of the example Jesus set for you to follow.

Who being God

Jesus' example of surrender _____

_____

_____

What must I do? _____

_____

_____

Made in the likeness of man

Jesus' example of surrender _____

_____

_____

What must I do? _____

_____

_____

Made Himself of no reputation

Jesus' example of surrender _____

_____

_____

What must I do? _____

_____

_____

Took upon Him the form of a servant

Jesus' example of surrender _____

_____

_____

What must I do? _____

_____

_____

Obedient unto death

Jesus' example of surrender _____

_____

_____

What must I do? _____

_____

_____

Let this mind be in you

Summarize the mind of Jesus_____

_____

_____

What must I do? _____

_____

_____

7. What areas of my life have I surrendered more completely to Him as a result of this study? _____

_____

_____

_____

ᴏ̃ **Time to Memorize:** Continue to review Philippians 2:5–8.

ᴏ̃ **Time for Prayer:** Take time to thank God for Who He is, for what He's done for you, and for the victory you can have in Him. Present yourself to God as a living sacrifice for His service.

From My Heart to Yours

This concludes our study of *A Life Surrendered*. We have seen that the Lord Jesus surrendered much when He came to this earth. He took on the likeness of man, humbled Himself in the form of a servant, and became obedient unto death.

You must ask yourself to what degree you have surrendered your life to the Lord Jesus. Are you His child? Have you accepted what He did for you on the cross of Calvary? His gracious death, burial, and resurrection were the final glory of His life on this earth—the whole purpose of His coming. Have you had a definite time in your life that you accepted what He did for you?

If you are saved, are you living a daily life that is fully surrendered to Him and to His will for you? How about the practical areas of your life that you have been challenged to surrender to Him?

Or are you living as if your life were your own? One day every knee will bow and every tongue will confess that He is Lord to the glory of God the Father. All will eventually surrender to Him. Knowing that one day we will stand in His presence, we have the choice to live our days here on earth for His glory. Which choice are you making today?

He calls us to a life surrendered to Him!

I Surrender All

All to Jesus I surrender,
All to Him I freely give;
I will ever love and trust Him,
In His presence daily live.

All to Jesus I surrender,
Humbly at His feet I bow;
Worldly pleasures all forsaken,
Take me, Jesus, take me now.

All to Jesus I surrender,
Make me, Savior, wholly Thine;
Let me feel Thy Holy Spirit,
Truly know that Thou art mine.

All to Jesus I surrender,
Lord, I give myself to Thee;
Fill me with Thy love and power,
Let Thy blessing fall on me.

I surrender all,
I surrender all,
All to Thee, my blessed Savior,
I surrender all.

—*Judson W. Van De Venter*[1]

Lesson 1

A Life Surrendered

[1]*The American Heritage Dictionary* (New York: American Heritage Publishing Co., 1973), 1925.

[2]*King James Study Bible* (Nashville: Thomas Nelson Publishers, 1981), 1850.

Lesson 2

Who Being God—His Riches

[1]J. Oswald Sanders, *The Incomparable Christ* (Chicago: Moody Press, 1971), 7.

[2]Ibid., 9.

[3]Henry Barraclough, "Ivory Palaces," *Majesty Hymns* (Greenville, S.C.: Majesty Music, 1996), 132.

[4]*King James Study Bible*, 1639.

[5]"Thou Who Wast Rich," *Christian Praise* (London: The Tyndale Press, 1957).

LESSON 3

Who Being God—His Birthright

[1] *King James Study Bible*, 1602.

[2] Ibid., 1645.

[3] Elisabeth Elliot, *Discipline: The Glad Surrender* (Grand Rapids, Mich.: Fleming H. Revell, 1982), 18.

[4] Sanders, 9.

[5] "Thou Who Wast Rich."

[6] Judy Wardell Halliday and Arthur W. Halliday, *Thin Within* (Nashville: W Publishing Group, 2002), 282.

LESSON 4

Made in the Likeness of Man—His Early Years

[1] Elliot, 89.

[2] Sanders, 22.

[3] Ibid., 27.

LESSON 5

Made in the Likeness of Man—His Humanity

[1] *King James Study Bible*, 1411.

[2] Sanders, 45.

LESSON 6

Made Himself of No Reputation—A Humble Occupation

[1] Sanders, 110.

[2] Ibid.

Lesson 7

Made Himself of No Reputation—A Humble Ministry

[1] *King James Study Bible*, 1966.

[2] Joseph Hart, "Come, Ye Sinners, Poor and Needy," *Majesty Hymns* (Greenville, S.C.: Majesty Music, 1996), 323.

Lesson 8

Took upon Him the Form of a Servant—A Servant's Heart

[1] *King James Study Bible*, 1592.

[2] Ron Hamilton, "Servant's Heart," *Majesty Hymns* (Greenville, S.C.: Majesty Music, 1996), 548.

Lesson 9

Took upon Him the Form of a Servant—A Servant's Actions

[1] *King James Study Bible*, 1637.

[2] Sanders, 109.

[3] Charles Law, Don Schultz, and Terry Parrish, *Jesus the Messiah, King of Israel* (Texarkana, Tex.: Baptist Sunday School Committee, 2001), 48.

Lesson 10

Obedient unto Death—Surrender of the Son

[1] King James Study Bible, 1524.

[2] Beth Moore, Jesus: the One and Only (Nashville, Tennessee: Broadman and Holman Publishers, 2002), 241.

[3] King James Study Bible, 1593.

[4] Sanders, 131.

[5] Strong's Expanded Exhaustive Concordance of the Bible (Nashville: Thomas Nelson Publishers, 2001), 2.

[6] King James Study Bible, 1818.

[7] Ibid., 1525.

[8]Ron Hamilton, "Abba, Father," Majesty Hymns, (Greenville, S.C.: Majesty Music, 1996), 426.

LESSON 11

Obedient unto Death—A Prayer of Surrender

[1]King James Study Bible, 1479.

[2]Moore, 244.

LESSON 12

My Life Surrendered

[1]Judson W. Van DeVenter, "I Surrender All," Majesty Hymns (Greenville: S.C.: Majesty Music, 1996), 390.